THE SUCCESS OF

Gordon H Chong + Associates

Other Books in the Success Series
Published by Walker and Company

*The Success of Caroline Jones Advertising,
Inc.: An Advertising Success Story,*
by Robert Fleming

The Success of Hispanic *Magazine:
A Publishing Success Story,*
by John García

*The Success of the Navajo Arts and
Crafts Enterprise: A Retail Success Story,*
by LeNora Begay Trahant

THE SUCCESS OF

Gordon H Chong + Associates

An Architecture Success Story

STEVEN A. CHIN

Photographs by Kim Komenich

WALKER AND COMPANY

NEW YORK

First published in the United States of America in 1996 by
Walker Publishing Company, Inc.

Published simultaneously in Canada by Thomas Allen & Son Canada,
Limited, Markham, Ontario

Library of Congress Cataloging-in-Publication Data
Chin, Steven A., 1959–
The success of Gordon H Chong + Associates: an architecture success story
/ Steven A. Chin; photographs by Kim Komenich.
p. cm.
Includes bibliographical references and index.
ISBN 0-8027-8307-4.—ISBN 0-8027-8308-2
1. Chong, Gordon H.—Juvenile literature. 2. Architects—
California—Biography—Juvenile literature. 3. Gordon H Chong +
Associates. [1. Chong, Gordon H. 2. Architects. 3. Chinese
Americans—Biography. 4. Gordon H Chong + Associates.]
I. Komenich, Kim, ill. II. Title.
NA737.C44C5 1995
720′.92—dc20
[B]   94-45155
CIP
AC

Printed in the United States of America

2 4 6 8 10 9 7 5 3 1

Contents

v

THE SUCCESS OF

Gordon H Chong + Associates

Architects use models to show clients what a building will look like.

Introduction: What Is Architecture?

Think back to this morning and retrace the steps you took as you got ready for the day. You probably got dressed in a bedroom, brushed your teeth in a bathroom, ate breakfast in a kitchen. Just imagine: Architects designed every room in your home. They determined its size, shape, and location; the number, size, and placement of closets, doors, and windows; the location of overhead lights, light switches, and electrical outlets. Architects even decided where the fixtures would be located in your bathroom.

Architects design other things besides houses. They lay out the gridwork of streets that define a city. They design schools, churches, hospitals, and offices.

The types of projects undertaken by architects reflect the needs of society. All societies need houses, streets, schools, and the like. In recent years, American architects have been designing more schools and health-care facilities. That's because two of the fastest-growing segments of our population are people under fifteen years old and those over sixty-five.

Clearly, architecture is a necessary and creative profession; it's also a business. The architect's job is to work with a client, or customer, to develop a design that meets the client's needs. After a design is agreed upon, the architect works with members of the building industry—carpenters, plumbers, and electricians—to transform the design into an actual structure. Being an architect is like being the conductor of a symphony orchestra. Both must try to get all the participants to perform their assigned tasks well and on time. Teamwork and good communication are essential.

1

Years ago, the architect was seen as the master builder, responsible for the total project. Today, the building industry has become more complex. Specialists in engineering, interiors, and other areas are now doing segments of projects once done by architects.

Architectural firms come in all shapes and sizes. Two-thirds of the firms in the United States are made up of five people or less, but they can range in size from just one or two architects to staffs of 100 or more. Each firm brings a unique combination of skills, interests, and values to its projects. Some firms specialize in designing family homes. Others focus on skyscrapers, schools, or hospitals.

Some firms are made up solely of architects. Each of the architects may have training in a special discipline, such as urban planning, interior design, or landscaping. Other firms employ not only architects but also a team of engineers—civil, structural, mechanical, and electrical (see glossary for definitions). Whatever their specialty, those involved in the architectural business say it is very exciting work.

Architecture is as much an artistic pursuit as it is an exercise in problem solving. It requires a sense of what looks good as well as a knowledge of what makes buildings stand up and stay up. When form and function come together, it is a job well done. In fact, architects say there is nothing more satisfying than the completion of a successful project.

When designing a structure, architects must also take other factors into consideration. Is the structure in keeping with the scale of the other structures in the neighborhood? How will it affect the flow of automobile traffic? Will there be adequate parking? Architects must also consider the building's impact on the environment. How energy efficient will the building be? Will it be constructed with man-made or natural materials?

Sometimes, structures are so beautifully designed that they become famous attractions. The gothic cathedrals of Europe and the hill dwellings of Greece are among the most impressive man-made structures in the world.

But fine architecture does not always have to come on a grand scale. It can just as well be a home or a restaurant. Sometimes it is a small detail that makes a room come alive, like a stream of sunlight passing through the windows and dancing off the walls. Maybe the natural wood floor draws you

Although this computer screen shows a complicated technical drawing, architects' work is also very artistic.

into the room. Or perhaps the airiness of the room makes you want to stay awhile.

As a young boy growing up in Honolulu, Hawaii, Gordon Chong noticed such architectural details as he helped his father design his family's new home. Gordon loved to draw and was encouraged to do so by his father. By the time he was in high school, he dreamed of becoming an architect and designing structures in which people would enjoy living and working.

After years of schooling, training, and traveling, Gordon became a licensed architect and was hired by an architectural firm in San Francisco, California. Seven years later, Gordon started his own company: Gordon H Chong + Associates. From a one-person firm, the company has grown to employ more than sixty people and has received larger and larger contracts to design airport terminals, hospitals, schools, and many other buildings.

Here is the story of how the architects at Gordon H Chong + Associates go about designing and building buildings.

Gordon H. Chong in the lobby of his firm's office.

· 1 ·

Gordon H Chong + Associates Architects/Engineers

As you step off the elevator into the headquarters of Gordon H Chong + Associates Architects/Engineers (GHC+A), you are immediately struck by the care that went into designing the space. The reception area has an elegant, professional, contemporary feel to it. The colors of the walls and carpet, the lighting, and the wood trim make the visitor feel welcome and comfortable. It is attention to these kinds of details that has made Gordon Chong successful at what he does.

Moving past the reception area, you come to a large, open space. Here architects and engineers seated behind drafting tables are busily working on their projects. The architects who designed this area gave a lot of thought to the specific needs of those individuals who would be using the space. As a result, the people who do the actual design work were assigned desks closest to the tall windows that run along the front and back of the building. The windows let in natural light and create an airiness that help them feel comfortable on the job.

One of the workers is architect Pauline Souza. Beginning on page 8 you'll find details on Pauline's background and her assessment of her job at GHC+A.

The offices of the managers, whose prime responsibilities are to oversee projects and employees, are located in the middle of the floor. These offices have no windows, but they do have sliding glass doors that look out into the main work areas. While the managers do not get as much natural light here as the rest of the staff, they benefit from having the privacy of small offices. Some key members of the management team, aside from Gordon himself, are John Ruffo, Linda Crouse, and Sam Edward Nunes. (More on these individuals in later chapters.)

Today, GHC+A has sixty-three people on staff. There are architects, engineers, draftsmen, receptionists, secretaries, accountants, and marketing people. Each plays an important role in making the firm run smoothly.

GHC+A has completed hundreds of projects, both large and small. The firm specializes in designing health-care facilities, schools, airports, and corporate interiors. Among the educational facilities for which the firm has been responsible are a magnet high school for the arts in San Francisco; thirty-four elementary schools throughout California; a dormitory for the University of California at Berkeley; gymnasiums for the college of Notre Dame in Belmont, California, and the Mt. Diablo Unified School District; and laboratories, health-care, and other facilities for Stanford University,

Even the parking structures GHC+A designs are beautiful!

TOOLS OF THE TRADE

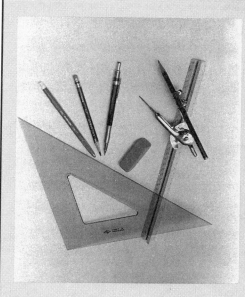

T square or parallel ruler
  For drawing straight and perpendicular lines.
Tracing paper
  For drawing, especially for quick ideas and overlays.
Scale or architectural "ruler"
  For drawing items to a specific scale or size.
Eraser (electric is ideal)
  For removing drawn lines.
Colored pencils, colored pastels, watercolors
  For making drawings.
Color pens
  For rendering quick ideas.
Compass
  For drawing curves, radii, or circles of different sizes.
Calculator
  For any math work.
Triangles
  For drawing angles.

Computers
Pencils with different lead types (F, H, B)
  Different leads produce darker or lighter line weights and can be used to give a drawing different contrasts.
Pencil sharpener (electric or manual)

the University of California Medical Center, and California State University. GHC+A has also created airport terminals, VIP lounges, and a flight kitchen for United Airlines; dining rooms and cafeterias for Bank of America and Splendido's restaurant in San Francisco, Fanny's Fish Market in Foster City, California, and the Nevada Air National Guard in Reno, Nevada, and health-care facilities for Kaiser Permanente in San Francisco.

PAULINE SOUZA

Age: 33
Place of Birth: Kowloon, Hong Kong
Educational Background: B.A. in architecture, University of California, Berkeley
Position: staff architect, focusing on public projects
Joined GHC+A: 1988

As a young child, Pauline knew she wanted to be an architect. She liked to draw. She was also influenced by the television show "The Brady Bunch," in which the father was an architect. "Although no one in my own family was an architect, my father encouraged me to draw, color, and sketch," she recalled.

Now that Pauline is an architect, she finds her job fun. "It's a challenge and an emotional charge for me," she said.

Pauline joined GHC+A because it offered her many opportunities to learn about architecture. She also felt encouraged to take on as much as she could. She liked the idea of working in project teams "small enough that I would get to do a lot."

Being a minority woman in a male-dominated profession has presented Pauline with numerous challenges. "I happen to be soft-spoken by nature, but many people believe I am this way because of my cultural background," she said. "Knowing this, I sometimes feel I have to force myself to speak louder and be more serious in formal situations."

As for being a woman, "I am expected to be understanding and compassionate, which can be an advantage with clients and a disadvantage with certain contractors," Pauline continued. "While I don't believe that women need to prove they can be 'manly,' I think that we have to work a little harder to show we are competent, logical, and strong willed. Luckily, architecture is a profession that encourages teamwork, which does much to break down stereotypes."

Pauline has worked in both minority-owned and white-owned firms. She believes that minority-owned firms sometimes have a competitive edge because they benefit from affirmative action programs. But as far as the work atmosphere in the office is concerned, she said, "the tone of the firm is set more by the owner's personality and philosophy than his or her ethnicity."

Pauline's first job was with a three-person firm. In a small office, each staff member does everything from going on site visits, typing up field reports, and writing up invoices to airbrushing illustrations. It was here that Pauline learned the meaning of teamwork and flexibility. There was a lot of emphasis on doing everything well and with care. "This concern for quality has greatly influenced how I approach my work," she said.

She is also appreciative of all the people who have challenged her to do more than she thought she could. She noted that she's worked with architects who "enjoyed passing on helpful information, like how to detail or present designs. In an apprenticeship like architecture, this [type of information] is critical."

But Pauline's key to success has been her passion for her work. "I believe strongly in architecture. I'm committed to doing quality work. I feel it's important to do good architecture that can affect people, even though they may not be aware of it.

"Good architecture is architecture that excites you, or comforts you, or challenges you—a built form that creates an emotion or tells a story. It's also important to notice small things—door handles, light fixtures, lobbies. It's exciting to find a small thing that's beautiful."

Open spaces and plenty of natural light make this environment a pleasant place to work.

And as GHC+A becomes more well known, its portfolio of work continues to expand. Gordon listens carefully to the needs of each client, so no two buildings are ever the same. "We believe in . . . architecture that responds to the specific location that we're in, the specific demands of the client, and the specific budget," explained Gordon. "It doesn't sound very unique, but what happens is all the projects look different."

Most recently, the firm received two prestigious awards: from the San Francisco chapter of the American Institute of Architects, an interior design award for the office building of the Bancroft-Whitney Publishing Company in San Francisco; and from the American Institute of Architecture-California Council, an urban design award for the Lady Shaw Senior Center in San Francisco's Chinatown.

While the Lady Shaw Senior Center is not an elaborate building, it fills a need, and that is one of the most important functions of good architecture.

The Lady Shaw Senior Center, which took eight years to complete, was not profitable for the firm, but it was a rewarding project for Gordon. It filled a need for low-cost housing for the elderly of the Asian community.

After nineteen years, Gordon H Chong + Associates is still considered a young firm. Many firms are between thirty and seventy years old. Gordon sees his firm's relatively young age as a benefit. While older firms become set in their ways, the direction of Gordon's firm is still flexible, so it will be able to take advantage of new opportunities as they arise.

How did GHC+A achieve the success it enjoys today? In large part it is due to the talents and determination of Gordon Chong himself. Let's take a closer look at this creative and successful individual.

11

Gordon knew success was not a sure thing when he started his own company, but he was willing to take a chance.

· 2 ·

Taking Risks

Some of the best things in life result from a willingness to take risks. And when you take risks, it helps to be well prepared. Gordon Chong was both when he decided to start his own architectural firm in 1976.

He had been working for a well-known San Francisco architectural firm, Whisler and Patri, since 1970. He rose through the ranks quickly, and by 1975 he had become one of the firm's top managers, sometimes called *principals*. At thirty-two years of age, he was rather young to be shouldering such responsibilities.

Until then, the idea of starting his own firm had not crossed Gordon's mind. Most architects who want to start their own companies wait until they are older, in order to gain more experience and to meet more potential clients. And besides, Gordon was a Chinese-American. At that time, very few successful architectural firms in the country were owned by Chinese-Americans or other minorities.

Still, Gordon felt he needed a change. He was unhappy at work and with each day grew increasingly frustrated. As vice president of operations, Gordon was one of the people responsible for setting the direction for the firm. But the firm had been around for decades, and its older principals were accustomed to doing things a certain way, and when Gordon pitched new ideas to them, those ideas were ignored.

After several months of this, Gordon decided that although the idea was scary, he was ready to venture out on his own. In 1976, he left Whisler and Patri and started a new company. He called his firm Gordon H Chong + Associates, even though he didn't yet have any associates working with him.

Many of Gordon's colleagues thought he was crazy to give up a top position at one of San Francisco's most established architectural firms. But Gordon had to follow his instincts. He was not sure that he would succeed, but he was determined to try his best. He felt prepared for the challenge, he was focused, and most important of all, he had lots of energy.

Gordon opened his office in an empty loft located in downtown San Francisco. Suddenly, he was not only the boss but the architect, secretary, errand boy, and janitor as well.

But there was no work for him to do. Gordon had no clients.

Had he made a terrible mistake? he wondered during those lonely times. Fortunately his brother, sister, and parents were just a phone call away. They would cheer Gordon up whenever he was feeling discouraged.

Gordon wasn't the only risk taker in the Chong family. In 1876, Gordon's grandfather, then just sixteen years old, traveled from Canton, China, to Hawaii. In return for his ocean passage, he agreed to work on a sugar plantation for five years. After his contract ended, Gordon's grandfather stayed in Hawaii and later married.

Gordon's father, Jerry, was born and raised in Hawaii. He, too, set off on a voyage. In 1925, when he was twenty-one, he traveled by ship to California, he enrolled at the University of California, Berkeley. There he studied fine arts and met Ruby Fung, a banking student. The two eventually married, and in the late 1920s they moved back to Honolulu, Hawaii. They had three children, Gerry, Jackie, and Gordon.

Jerry loved to paint, but to support his family he took a job as the art director of the *Honolulu Advertiser,* the local newspaper. He did not let his full-time job at the newspaper stop him from painting, however. On weekends, he would wake up at dawn, load his easel and tattered box of oil paints into his convertible, and head out to the scenic hills around Honolulu. He painted sunrises and beach and mountain scenes. By the time he returned

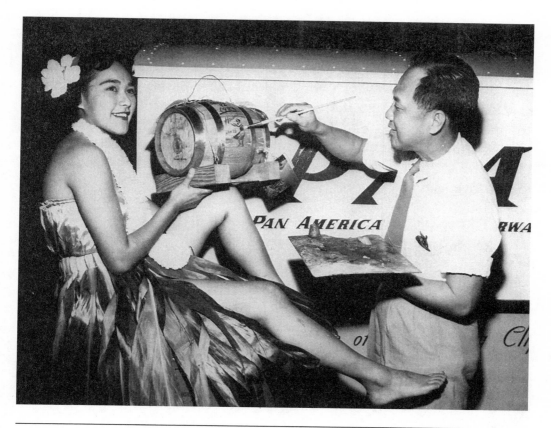

Gordon's father worked in advertising to support his family.

home, the rest of the family would just be climbing out of bed to start their day.

Gordon's parents exposed their children to many different activities, both cultural and athletic. They took the children to the symphony and opera. They gave them lessons of all kinds, including swimming, horseback riding, ballroom dancing, and piano. They took them on trips to the U.S. mainland. In 1954, when Gordon was eleven years old, the family took a trip to the South to visit Mississippi and Louisiana. At one point in their travels there, they came across two drinking fountains side by side. The sign

15

above one fountain read "Colored"; the other sign read "Whites." "We didn't know which one to use," Gordon recalled.

Influenced by his father, Gordon developed a love of art. He liked to draw and would sometimes accompany his father on his weekend painting trips. It was during these short excursions that Jerry would teach Gordon about art and drawing.

"My father was the single most influential individual in my early career," says Gordon. "He shared his passion with me and instilled, early on, the focus, drive, and energy it takes to be an architect."

A young Gordon and his family pose with Grandma.

The Chong family's new home was a combination of ideas from father and son.

"The Chinese have a saying, *Tien, di, ren,*" his father would tell Gordon, explaining that good composition consisted of three components. "There's something big in the sky, something low—the earth—and something in the middle—man." Jerry saw color and composition in everything, so Gordon was brought up looking at things more closely than the average person.

When Gordon was six, his parents decided to build a new home. Jerry Chong would design it. Every weekend for months, the family would drive around Honolulu looking at houses that were for sale to get architectural ideas for the new Chong house.

To help prepare for a career in architecture, take the following classes in elementary and high school:

Drawing, painting, watercolor, art classes (history or other)—to learn about color and form in two dimensions.

Geometry—to learn to apply math to space and shapes.

Photography

Sculpture—to learn about form in three dimensions.

Automechanics—to learn how things work and are assembled. Aids in envisioning three dimensions.

Computer graphics

Recommended college courses include structural theory, color theory, model building, CAD, construction materials and methods, art history, urban design, and life drawing.

As they drove from one house to the next, Gerry and Jackie quickly got bored. To them, the houses looked pretty much the same. "Do we have to go to *another* house?" they would whine to their father. They would much rather have been playing at the beach.

But Gordon loved visiting the houses that were up for sale, and his interest did not go unnoticed. His father encouraged Gordon to talk about what he liked about each particular house. His father used some of the ideas in designing their house.

The Chongs' new house took a year to build. When it was finally completed, Gordon was as proud as his father. He felt he had contributed to its creation, down to the small waterfall surrounded by tropical ferns in the backyard. He and his father had collected the stones and built it together.

In middle school, Gordon enjoyed carpentry shop and metal shop because he liked using his hands to build things. Then in high school, he discovered mechanical drawing. As his talents emerged, Gordon's father encouraged him to consider architecture as a profession.

Not only was Gordon attracted to school courses that were related to architecture and engineering, he also enjoyed team sports.

In 1960, after graduating from high school, seventeen-year-old Gordon started classes at the University of Oregon. He soon discovered that Eugene, Oregon, was worlds apart from Honolulu. Of course, the weather was different—he had expected that—but so were the customs, the people, and even the way people spoke English.

One of the biggest challenges for Gordon was getting used to the fact that most people in Eugene were white and of European extraction; they were not accustomed to being around Chinese-Americans. In Hawaii, on the other hand, most of the people were Pacific Islanders or Asian, with roots in Japan, the Philippines, and China.

Being one of the few Chinese-Americans at the University of Oregon was sometimes difficult for Gordon. In Hawaii, Gordon was treated like everyone else, but here people treated him differently. They would assume that Gordon was a foreigner because he was not white. Some would say to him, "Hey, you can speak English fairly well for a Chinese." Of course, Gordon, like most Americans, had spoken English his entire life.

19

The discrimination was difficult for Gordon to understand. His brother had joined a fraternity and his sister a sorority at their colleges in California. Gordon wanted to do the same. But when he tried to join one of the fraternities on the University of Oregon campus, he was turned away because of his race.

Feeling like a social outcast, Gordon concentrated on his studies. He spent most of his time doing classwork and in time made friends with other students at the School of Architecture. He and his friends would spend long nights in the school's studios working on architectural projects. They would design structures and then make cardboard models of buildings to present to their teachers. It was hard but satisfying work.

In 1963, Richard Smith, one of Gordon's professors in the architecture school, brought Gordon and several other students to Japan to study and draw Japanese buildings. The simplicity and beauty of Japanese architecture impressed Gordon. It reinforced his love of architecture and his commitment to this career. Later that year, Gordon spent four months traveling and studying different architectural styles. He visited the Middle East, Punjab in northern India, Greece, western Europe, and Scandinavia. Day after day he walked through cities, taking in village squares, churches, cathedrals, and castles. To document his trip, he took photographs and drew in a sketchbook.

"Traveling simply widened my exposure and heightened my awareness of the environment around me," he says. "After traveling, I saw spaces and details differently, and I was much more sensitized to all aspects of the built and unbuilt environment."

After graduating from the University of Oregon in 1966, Gordon joined the United States Coast Guard for reserve duty and then attended Edinburgh University in Scotland. He studied town planning and low-cost housing. Gordon was particularly interested in worker housing. He went to Scotland in order to study with experts in this area. In 1968, he received a master's degree in architecture.

After Gordon finished his schooling, he received a job offer from a firm in Boston. But Gordon's siblings, who lived in California, persuaded him to move to San Francisco. In San Francisco, Gordon was hired by an architect named John Field. He worked with Field for two years and then went to Whisler and Patri. He worked there for seven years until he left to start his own firm in 1976.

Now he was entirely on his own, with no staff and no clients.

Gordon tries to support and encourage his staff, treating them as though they are part of a big family.

· 3 ·

Making Progress

For Gordon, starting his own business was the most exciting thing he had ever done. He would spend his daytime hours trying to find new clients. Then at night he would take his seat behind his drafting table and work on the only projects he had at that time—single-family-home re-modeling. (See pages 24–25 on how to read a blueprint.) At about ten o'clock each night, Gordon would take a break from drawing and would build furniture for his office for several hours. Since he did not have enough money to buy furniture, he built his own desks and bookshelves and even constructed a large conference table.

Gordon usually got home after midnight and crawled into bed exhausted. At six o'clock in the morning, he would get up and start over again. This routine lasted for several years while Gordon was building his business.

Gordon discovered that his office space was a hindrance to business. For one thing, it was a large, open area that would get cold and drafty during the winter. (The building had no heat.) There were also cracks in the walls. Under these unattractive conditions, Gordon found it was hard to impress potential clients. Some would come up to visit Gordon and see the sparse office filled with homemade furniture and then decide against hiring him.

After a short time as a solo practitioner—as architects who work on their own are called—Gordon got a lucky break. His old firm called him one day and asked if he would be interested in working as a consultant.

Two of Gordon's old projects at Whisler and Patri were still not finished. Since he knew the most about them, the firm was willing to pay Gordon to

HOW TO READ A BLUEPRINT

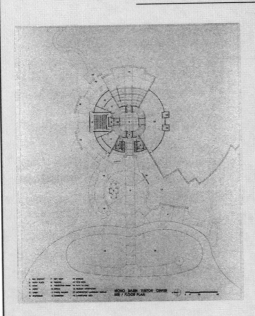

Drawings are the primary way architects and engineers explain how they want to see their building constructed. These drawings indicate to the contractors, electricians, plumbers, and others how to assemble the building.

Construction drawings, or working drawings, are generally produced through a process called blueprinting. A blueprint can have a dark blue background and white lines or, more commonly, dark blue or black lines against a white background.

The size of the sheets of paper can vary, though the standard size is twenty-four by thirty-six inches or thirty by forty-two inches. The size of the drawing often depends on the size of the building itself. The larger the drawing, the more detail that can be shown. But if drawings are too large, they may be hard to carry around at the construction site. In this case they are reduced by 50 percent.

Off to the side of a given drawing, there is a lot of information: the scale of the drawing, the date the drawing was originally printed and when any revisions were made, the name of the architect or engineer of record, the name of the project and/or the owner, the name of the drawing, such as "classroom," and the sheet number in the series.

Through the use of different symbols, the architect illustrates the kind of materials and systems that will be used in the building. There are directional symbols indicating north, east, south, and west; symbols for electrical and plumbing fixtures; as well as symbols for structural connections. These symbols are sometimes identified in a box, called a legend, located somewhere on the page.

Construction drawings may come in a set. Each drawing may be related to a different type of work required to complete the project. For instance, there may be separate plans for demolition, landscape, architecture, and the various engineering components—mechanical, electrical, and structural. In addition, there may be a fire-safety plan.

A typical set of blueprints contains the following:

Site plan. This sheet shows the topography of the project site. It may illustrate the elevation of the earth and any contours in the land. Sometimes these drawings will indicate sidewalks, fencing, and paved areas.

Landscape plan. This sheet is generally one of the first in the set. It shows the vegetation, both existing and new, on the project site. Other landscape features may also be shown, such as lighting and irrigation systems.

Architectural plan. These drawings depict the new construction, usually beginning with floor plans and moving to more detailed drawings of wall sections and even door and window details.

Structural plan. This set of drawings shows the structures, such as column and beams, that are needed to support the walls and floors of a building.

Mechanical plan. These drawings detail the heating, ventilating, and air-conditioning systems of a building. The ducts, piping, and plumbing may be shown here.

Electrical plan. This sheet shows the electrical wiring and the location of light fixtures and outlets that will be needed on a building or house.

Plumbing plan. These drawings show the location of the plumbing fixtures (sinks, toilets, etc.) as well as the piping for hot and cold water.

When each of these plans is completed, in combination with specifications detailing the type of materials to be used, the end result is a structure—a man-made creation representing the needs and vision of a client, the talent of architects and engineers, and the skills of the contractors.

Communicating with people is one of Gordon's strengths: He learned early on in his career that the more people you meet, the more potential clients you will have.

help complete them. One was a housing project for senior citizens, and the other was a Wendy's restaurant. Gordon could not afford to refuse their offer of work.

Gordon's company grew very slowly. As a businessman, Gordon was conservative. When he did not get enough work during a particular month to pay the bills, he dipped into his savings from his old job, rather than asking a bank for a loan.

Gordon didn't bring in other partners to help him, although the name of the firm, Gordon H Chong + Associates, implied that there was more than one person. For laughs, Gordon's friends would call Gordon's office late at night and ask to speak to an associate. One Christmas, his friends gave Gordon a set of store mannequins so that he would have some "associates" in his office.

After working at a large architectural firm for seven years, Gordon had experience working on large, expensive projects for big corporations. Being an optimist, he thought he would get the same kind of work on his own. He soon discovered that big corporations did not want to hire a solo practitioner.

But Gordon never gave up. He believed that if he kept working hard and producing good work, business would improve. Fortunately, he had a lot of enthusiasm and no family demands. He was able to pour all his energy into building up his business.

Eventually, Gordon learned where to find new clients and how to attract them. He started talking to old clients and getting them to introduce him to other people. He also became involved in community activities, something he had learned from one of his old bosses, Piero Patri. Gordon got appointed to the Berkeley planning commission. He joined the board of directors of several local arts groups and neighborhood community groups. He joined a professional group, the American Institute of Architects, and he was a founding member, and second president, of the Asian American Architects and Engineers. Now Gordon was spending three to four nights a week attending social functions and meeting people. His new involvements added to his already hectic schedule, but they would soon start to pay off.

In 1978 Gordon was hired by the Bank of America, one of the largest banks in California. It was a major client. Gordon was asked to plan the interior spaces for the bank's offices in San Francisco and to design a large cafeteria for its employees.

After proving himself on that job, business began to pick up. Gordon got more jobs with large corporations, planning new office spaces and redesigning older offices. As more work came in, he could finally hire some associates.

Within two years, GHC+A grew from one person to five persons. It outgrew its old, drafty space.

Gordon moved the firm to a bigger office space on 121 Second Street in San Francisco. He also hired five more people to handle the increasing workload.

GORDON H. CHONG, FAIA

AGE: 52
PLACE OF BIRTH: Honolulu, Hawaii
EDUCATIONAL BACKGROUND: B.A. in architecture, University of Oregon; M.A. in architecture, Edinburgh University, Scotland
POSITION: Head of Gordon H Chong + Associates, which he started in 1976

Gordon enjoys the entire process of architecture, from dealing with the client and creating a design to watching the building being built.

"That's satisfaction—to start with a blank sheet of paper, and then to see the thing actually built." When it's completed, you say, 'Wow, look at that. I created *that!*' "

When Gordon isn't supervising projects he is on the phone looking for new projects to work on and trying to solve clients' problems. When it comes to the actual architectural work, Gordon especially enjoys participating in the design at the conceptual level as well as visiting construction sites when his schedule permits.

Gordon gets his drive to succeed from his family. His mother and father, brother, and sister supported his efforts from the beginning. In 1983 Gordon wed Dorian Kingman, and the couple now have two daughters, Phoenix and Kaitlin.

He tries to bring the notion of a strong family to his business. "I talk about trust in terms of family, which, I think, comes from my

Asian background," he said. "I treat the office members more like an extended larger family. I say that because I think families trust each other. But . . . you can't always guarantee everybody employment. . . . So it's different from a mom-and-pop family grocery store, but I still call it a family."

Even though Gordon's firm has been successful, the company must still overcome the perception that it receives special treatment from the government—such as getting hired on public projects just because it is Asian owned and not because of the quality of the firm's work. (Through government's affirmative action programs, minority-owned firms are given the first opportunity to be hired on public projects.)

"We have benefited from a lot of those [affirmative action] programs, but it also creates a stigma in how majority firms see you and stereotype you without knowing how good or how bad you are," said Gordon. For example, some people mistakenly believe that a minority-owned firm must be small and lacking in capability. "So af-firmative action programs are a mixed blessing. After a certain point you need to be recognized for being a professional."

But despite the drawbacks, Gordon believes that a minority-owned firm needs the help of an affirmative action program. "I would like to compete without it," he said, "but the reality is it's hard to compete without it. In five or ten years, I want to be recognized as a first-class firm, so that I don't have to depend on preferences. I just want to do it on the merits of our own firm. I don't want people to think there's a stigma about the quality of work because we are a minority firm. That's a real problem to overcome. I think a lot of minorities feel you have to give 150 percent just to be seen as equal."

Gordon especially enjoys taking on health-care projects. "I like the end results of helping the patients and the doctors," said Gordon. "To walk through a hospital and see the patients and how an environment affects the healing process is rewarding."

Gordon also likes designing facilities for schools for similar reasons. He believes a comfortable classroom environment not only improves students' abilities to learn better and more quickly but also helps relieve stress.

According to Gordon, if there is a drawback to the profession, it's that architecture is not high paying. "That's the downside of it—seeing attorneys make what they make and doctors make what they make, then seeing what contributions we make to the value of a piece of property and being compensated so little for it," he said. "We knock ourselves out trying to do good work, and sometimes the general public doesn't appreciate it."

But he added, "If you're only into it for the money, then you've chosen the wrong profession. . . . you should be able to make a decent living and still be able to enjoy doing architecture."

For his contributions toward advancing his profession, Gordon was admitted to the American Institute of Architects' College of Fellows. It is the AIA's highest honor. Only 5 percent (2,200) of its 55,000 members are fellows of which only 170 are minorities.

When Gordon had first started, he had not given much thought to how large his firm eventually would be. Now he had to start thinking about its future. Did he want his firm to remain small or to grow?

During those early years of the firm, Gordon would sometimes turn to Pat Bell, a longtime friend and business consultant, for advice. Pat had much more experience in the management of architectural business and had helped Gordon rise through the ranks at his old firm. Pat advised him, "If you enjoy working on bigger projects, then you must continue to grow."

Gordon, who liked the challenge of larger, more complex projects, agreed. He had learned the hard way that large corporate clients were more comfortable working with larger architectural firms.

Pat also stressed that if Gordon's company was to be successful as a large firm, he had to develop strong management. Pat urged Gordon to share not

When GHC+A began to grow, Pat Bell, an experienced business consultant, offered Gordon helpful advice.

only the design work but the management tasks as well. Again Gordon agreed. He realized that he could not continue to do everything himself.

Gordon made another important decision about the direction his firm would take. As he talked with more and more people about architecture, he discovered that not everyone could define "good architecture," but they all could define "good service." So Gordon decided that his firm would focus on providing quality service to clients. Of course, architectural design would still be very important, but Gordon wanted his firm to develop a reputation for excellent service.

Expansion included the addition of a marketing department at GHC+A.

· 4 ·

Expansion

Business at GHC+A improved sharply after Gordon hired Linda Crouse as director of marketing in 1983. Her job was to assist Gordon in organizing the business and bringing in more work for the firm.

At the time Linda Crouse was hired, the concept of a marketing manager was a pretty new one for most architectural firms. And in a firm as small as GHC+A, the main architects usually did all the marketing.

Generally, architects bill their clients for the number of hours they spend working on their projects. This is how the firms get the money to pay their architects. Marketing staff, however, are not billable—that is, their time is not charged to the clients. Thus, small firms usually cannot afford to keep a marketing director on staff.

But at Gordon's firm, hiring a marketing person soon proved to be a good idea. Linda quickly became an expert on the laws that give minority-owned companies preference in public projects. The San Francisco Human Rights Commission gave preference points, or bonus points, to minority-owned architectural firms and building companies during the bidding process. This system also encouraged nonminority firms to team up with minority-owned firms in seeking public projects.

With Linda's help, GHC+A was suddenly getting the opportunity to work on large city projects. GHC+A became part of a team of architectural firms working on the expansion of San Francisco's huge convention center, known as the Moscone Center.

LINDA CROUSE

AGE: 34
PLACE OF BIRTH: Camden, New Jersey
EDUCATIONAL BACKGROUND: B.A. in city planning, Rutgers University, New Brunswick, New Jerey
POSITION: director of marketing
JOINED GHC+A: 1983

Linda previously worked as an assistant to the marketing coordinator at another architectural firm. She had started there as an administrative assistant, and then moved up the ranks. But people there continued to view her as a secretary. "I wanted more of a say," Linda recalled.

She thought it was interesting that a small firm like GHC+A was looking for a full-time marketing person. It indicated to her that Gordon was willing to take a risk.

With seven employees, Gordon realized he needed to start hiring people to help manage the business. In search of someone energetic and trustworthy, Gordon hired Linda. Today, Linda's role is to direct the marketing efforts of the firm, as well as to help set its general goals.

"I get involved in every project we are pursuing and oversee the proposals, graphics, photography, and public relations—anything that has a public side to it," she said.

Linda appreciates the experience she has gained at GHC+A. Since joining the firm, she has been promoted to a principal and director of marketing. She feels she brings a balance to the firm's management team because she's younger than the others, she is a nontechnical person, and she's a woman.

Because GHC+A is a relatively young firm, there isn't any one person who feels he or she knows all the answers. "Gordon's tendency is to always give people responsibility and try to support them," Linda said. "A lot of responsibility is given to younger people on design and management issues. Gordon wants people in the firm to succeed and wants the firm to succeed. In order for that to happen, you have to have trust and you have to be able to share information."

Linda believes the key to her success has been "a lot of energy and dedication. I mean I worked really hard." Gordon has served as both her teacher and source of inspiration. As Linda explained, "Gordon has taught me a lot in different areas—certainly in dealing diplomatically with people. . . . Gordon is an inspiration in the sense that he has worked hard to get the firm where it is. He's really created a firm out of nothing. The changes are really pretty dramatic thinking back to when I joined the company and where we are now. So that's an inspiration. Hard work pays off."

Linda also has some very good friends who are involved in marketing who have given her different ideas and opportunities and with whom she discusses her ideas.

Linda continues to work at GHC+A because she is respected, she's given a lot of responsibility, and she enjoys working for Gordon. "He really doesn't have secrets," she said. "There are a lot of companies that don't share a lot of information with their staff.

"You can pretty much get involved in whatever you want, if you show an interest. I think we're always changing, always trying to find new things in order to improve. That gives you additional challenges."

Expanding GHC+A enabled the firm to hire more architects, and interns who hope to become architects.

Linda also developed filing and recordkeeping systems to manage all of the firm's information, including graphics and photographs of past projects. This made it much easier for Gordon and her to produce proposals when seeking new projects. The better the proposals and presentations, the better the firm's chance of getting hired for the job.

Gordon now began to focus on attracting certain types of clients. These included large corporations, public agencies, and educational institutions such as universities. The three groups had several characteristics in common. They were usually fiscally conservative with large bureaucracies that required any architectural firm they hired to possess strong management skills and offer good customer service. In addition, most were committed to working with minority firms.

Gordon also began exploring the opportunities for health-care projects. He knew that architectural projects in this field had been slow over the last ten years and thought that work might begin to pick up soon.

In deciding whether to take the jump into the health-care field, Gordon and Linda determined what it would take to enter this market and whether it would be worth the effort. Did they have enough money and energy to enter and stay in this market for a while, even if they did not get work right away? Did they have the experience and skills to compete for health-care projects?

They decided it was worth a try. As a minority-owned company, Gordon's firm was eligible for affirmative action programs at both the state and federal levels. Its first project in health care was for California's Napa State Hospital.

Using the firm's minority status, Gordon and Linda arranged several partnerships with larger architectural firms that had expertise in the area of health care. In this way, GHC+A became involved in projects at San Francisco General Hospital and Laguna Honda Hospital, also in San Francisco.

Suddenly, the size of the projects the firm was handling had grown enormously. Before taking advantage of the affirmative action programs, GHC+A had been working on relatively small projects with construction budgets ranging from $100,000 to $1.2 million. Now, the firm was overseeing projects with construction budgets of $5 million to $40 million.

Gordon conferring with Sam Nunes, architect and senior associate at GHC+A.

· 5 ·

Making Changes

In 1986, Gordon made two decisions that had a great impact on GHC+A. First, he decided to move the firm to an even larger office. It was located in a nicer section of downtown San Francisco on Maiden Lane. Not only was the new office bigger, it was much more attractive. It was intended to impress clients.

The second decision was an unusual and somewhat risky business move for an architectural firm of GHC+A's size: Gordon began hiring engineers. Until then, the firm had been composed only of architects. If an engineer was needed to design the structural, electrical, air-conditioning, or heating system for a project, Gordon would find one outside the firm to do the job.

Besides the health-care projects, the firm had been doing a lot of renovation work, which requires engineers. By hiring his own engineers, Gordon would now have greater control over the renovation projects and they could move ahead more quickly.

Today, eleven engineers work at Gordon H Chong + Associates. Five specialize in designing electrical systems; three work on mechanical systems; and three design the frames and structures that keep a building standing. Several, like Bob Riegel, the first engineer to join the firm, have degrees and licenses in both architecture and engineering. This means that these people can do architectural design when there is no engineering work to do.

Adding engineers to an architectural firm presented several challenges. Architects think and work one way, while engineers think and work another way. One of Bob's jobs was to help the two groups better understand each other.

It has not been an easy task. Architects are used to working with paper, surrounded with ideas and images. "They work through the process until they hit upon a solution," Bob said. "Sometimes they work partway through a problem and find that they have to back up and go at it in an entirely different way. It is a creative process."

On the other hand, he said, engineers take a much more scientific approach to their work. They use mathematical equations to get precise answers and measurements. For these reasons, the two groups do not always see eye to eye when it comes to solving problems.

GHC+A's new, bigger space is good for creative work and good for business.

Beginning in 1987, Gordon's next major move was to hire people with expertise in designing educational and health-care facilities. He hired architect Charles Higueras to go after the education market in northern California. Then he hired John Ruffo, a principal from a major San Francisco firm specializing in the area of health care.

The new hires eventually led to getting three major health-care projects. The first was the Veterans Administration Drug and Alcohol Rehabilitation facility in Menlo Park, California, a $27 million project. The other two were

Gordon is sharing more of the responsibilities of running the firm with other employees under GHC+A's new organizational structure.

JOHN RUFFO

AGE: 41
PLACE OF BIRTH: San Jose, California
EDUCATIONAL BACKGROUND: B.A. in architecture, California Polytechnic State University, San Luis Obispo; M.A. in architecture, University of California, Berkeley
POSITION: managing principal
JOINED GHC+A: 1992

When John started college he chose biology as his major with the intention of getting a graduate degree in marine biology. Then in the summer of 1972, John and one of his friends from high school who was an architectural student at the University of California, Berkeley, built a house together in a small community just outside Yosemite National Park. "We were carpenters, and I really enjoyed it," recalled John. "I thought architecture would be an interesting blend of science and creativity. At that point, I decided I would go back to school and go into architecture."

John still enjoys science and learning about science through his building projects. In addition to the health-care projects that he's handled, he's worked on a wildlife center at the Coyote Point Museum in San Mateo and a research facility in the Antarctic.

Before coming to GHC+A, John worked for Anshen & Allen for almost sixteen years, the last eight years as a managing principal. Anshen & Allen had gone from twenty-five people in one office to

145 people in three offices. "It was a very large corporate firm, and becoming more and more corporate," recalled John. "I felt I had learned a lot, and I was looking for an opportunity to develop a greater degree of autonomy and get away from the politics of a big firm."

John had known Gordon for some time through the American Institute of Architects. He was considering starting his own firm and sought Gordon's advice. At the end of a two-hour lunch conversation, Gordon asked John if he'd be interested in joining GHC+A as a partner.

The two architects discovered that they had many of the same values and goals. They both believed architects should have the greatest respect for the client and provide high-quality service.

"We are both interested in design, but not interested in being a 'design boutique' architectural firm," John said. "That means neither of us have the desire to become a 'star' design firm that gets a lot of press and attention. I think we strive for a quality product that's at the cutting edge of the profession, both in the way we do the work and in what the end results are."

John believes his management style complements Gordon's. Whereas Gordon has been operating as a sole proprietor for nineteen years, John understands the dynamics of a larger firm.

John's role at GHC+A has evolved from mainly building up the health-care market to working on financial planning, budgeting, and marketing. He's also involved in handling operational tasks, such as personnel evaluations and salary reviews, incentive programs, overall office staffing, and computer applications.

All these responsibilities have taken him away from actual designing. He continues to work with clients, however, helping them to make design decisions. In addition, he helps his colleagues get ready for meetings with clients. For instance, he'll pose design questions he thinks the clients might raise. As John summed it up, he puts in place "the organization, the environment, the staff, and the resources that allow good design to occur."

It's obvious from John's success in the field that he is personally motivated to succeed, but it's also important that he have fun at what he does. "I don't want it to be drudgery," he said. "I want to look forward to coming to work every day."

According to John, the staff at GHC+A "enjoy working together . . . [and] are growing in their responsibilities and capabilities." He believes architectural firms must grow in order to survive. "If not, you lose good people because good people want to have [an] opportunity [to grow]," he said.

John's overall assessment: "Although GHC+A is not succeeding on every front, we're accomplishing enough so that it's rewarding. There's still . . . a lot to do, but there's still plenty of fun to be had."

a $45 million project and a $68 million project for the health-care company Kaiser Permanente.

To get these projects, GHC+A had to compete with the largest architectural health-care firms in the nation. The other firms had hundreds of photographs of their prior projects to show off. Gordon's firm had completed only a couple of small projects.

By 1989, GHC+A had outgrown most of the federal and local minority affirmative action programs. Many of the programs are restricted to firms that make no more than $2.5 million in any given year. Suddenly, Gordon found his firm had to compete against international firms that had anywhere from 400 to 1,000 people working for them.

The firm had also outgrown its Maiden Lane office, so in May 1989 it moved into its current offices at 130 Sutter Street.

In 1993, Gordon realized that in order for the company to grow and evolve, he needed more help in managing the firm. It was time to share the responsibility of owning and running his company. He made John Ruffo a managing partner, as well as a shareholder in GHC+A.

As a partner, John is expected to bring in more work for the firm as well as to represent GHC+A to clients. "Clients want to feel like they're being taken care of by a principal of the firm," John said.

In the firm's new structure, Linda Crouse and Geoff Adams, director of public works, were named principals, and architects Sam Nunes and Charles Higueras were named senior associates. With their new titles, these individuals accepted greater responsibility in helping to manage the firm. They have met the challenge to come up with more ideas and new strategies for GHC+A. In the end, all of these changes should result in more work and profit.

The Mono Basin National Forest Scenic Area Visitor Center.

· 6 ·

Cathedral in the Wild

A country of wonderful contrasts, hot deserts bordered by snow-laden mountains, cinders and ashes scattered on glacier-polished pavement, frost and fire working in the making of beauty.

—John Muir, describing the Mono Basin
during his first summer in the Sierra

One of the most spectacular places of natural beauty in the eastern Sierra Nevada mountains is Mono Lake. It is an immense inland sea surrounded by nonactive volcanoes on three sides. On the fourth side lies an endless tract of sagebrush desert.

Twice the size of San Francisco, the blue saltwater lake stretches thirteen miles east to west, and eight miles north to south. Created about one million years ago, Mono is one of the oldest bodies of water in North America.

Mono means "flies" in the language of the Yokuts, the Native Americans who live to the south of this region. The Native Americans who lived in the Mono Basin—the Kuzedika, or the Mono Lake Paiute—collected the abundant alkali fly pupae, or kutsavi, and used them as one of their main food sources. They also used the kutsavi to trade with the Yokuts for acorns. The U.S. Cavalry obtained the name for the area from its Yokut scouts.

The most unusual features of Mono are the mushrooming rocks and knobby spires formed by the high calcium content of the lake water. These formations, known as *tufa*, appear to be from another world.

This was the setting for one of GHC+A's most interesting building projects—the Mono Basin National Forest Scenic Area Visitor Center.

Throughout the 1970s, the water level of Mono Lake had been steadily dropping a foot or more each year because the city of Los Angeles had been taking water from the streams that feed the lake. Unless something was done soon, the lake was doomed. In 1978, appalled by this prospect, environmentalist David Gaines and a group of concerned individuals—the Mono Lake Committee—began talking to legislators and concerned Californians to see if anything could be done to save the lake.

The controversy surrounding the Mono Lake basin—environmental interests clashed with the water-supply needs of farmers and Los Angeles residents—began to attract people to the lake. People were curious to see what they were reading about in the newspapers. As more and more visitors came, the U.S. Forest Service recognized the need for a visitor center that could present the story of the lake to the public. The center would also explain to visitors the history of the land and its native people, the Kuzedika, also called the Mono Lake Paiute.

In September 1984, Congress passed the California Wilderness Act, creating the Mono Basin National Forest Scenic Area. It was intended to protect the ecosystems of Mono Lake and the surrounding basin. The law also allowed the construction of a visitor center by the U.S. Forest Service. To help plan the center, the service created an advisory committee. Members of

Tufa (pronounced too-fah): These tower formations were created when freshwater springs containing calcium bubbled up through the carbonate-rich lake water. The mixture of these waters produced calcium carbonate, a white limestone deposit that formed the unusual spires and knobs.

As the architects intended, the Mono Lake Visitor Center blends in with the natural beauty of the region.

this committee included the supervisor of the U.S. Forest Service, a representative from the California State Beaches and Parks Department, a representative of the Los Angeles Department of Water and Power, and David Gaines.

After careful investigation, the U.S. Forest Service selected a twenty-acre site one mile west of Mono Lake. A land exchange was arranged with the city of Los Angeles Department of Water and Power, giving the U.S. Forest Service ownership of the parcel. The site offered a view of the entire basin. From the center's windows and walkways, visitors would be able to see the lake, its islands, the volcanic craters, and the Sierra Nevada and White Mountains.

By 1987, the U.S. Forest Service was looking for an architecture firm to help build the visitor center. The U.S. Forest Service was already familiar

Bob Sandusky and Gary Jereczek hike around the Mono Lake area. The visitor center was built on the site of a garbage dump.

with the work of GHC+A. The firm had previously helped the service conduct an analysis of earthquake damage at some of its facilities, remodeled the interiors of its San Francisco office, and designed several small buildings in other forests in California.

Before hiring GHC+A, the U.S. Forest Service had completed a number of preliminary stages of work. Bob Sandusky, one of the staff architects for the Forest Service, had developed some design concepts and brought them to the advisory committee for review and approval. He had also prepared a report detailing the needs of visitors to the center and how the structure should function. For example, the report listed the activities that would be performed in the building, how many people would use the facility, what machinery or equipment would be needed, and anything else that would affect the size or design of the project.

Sandusky determined that the center would be the single most important location for educating the public about the scenic area. The U.S. Forest Service wanted a theater, a library, and an exhibit hall. The center would house a permanent photography exhibit, called the "Moods of Mono," with works of Ansel Adams and other famous photographers of the region. The U.S. Forest Service also wanted a store and a conference room.

Sandusky had also done an environmental impact report to determine the effect a visitor center might have on the neighboring area. For instance, because the Mono Basin was such an environmentally sensitive area, some people did not even want the center near Mono Lake. They feared that the increased traffic might hurt the lake. Others wondered whether a visitor center would attract too many people and thus destroy the peace and serenity of the nearby town of Lee Vining.

Lee Vining, California. Mono Lake can be seen in the distance.

• • •

The next stage was to draw sketches of the center. The sketches would help establish the basic form and size of the structure and its location on the site. The primary purpose of these drawings was to analyze various design possibilities and estimate the cost of the center.

When making drawings of this type, an architect may include bubble designs. In a library, for instance, one bubble may represent the bookshelves, and the bubble next to it may represent the librarian's desk. The architect can move the bubbles around in search of their most logical positions—in other words, the arrangement that will make the building operate efficiently. By moving things around, the architect is able to establish what the flow of human traffic might be.

The architect may also draw thumbnail sketches on rolls of tracing paper using a felt-tipped pen. In the beginning, these small drawings are very rough, but as they progress, the drawings become more precise.

Bob Sandusky's conceptual design was based on the ideas of many different people. He talked to community groups, landscape architects, the district ranger, his U.S. Forest Service colleagues, the Mono Lake and the advisory committees, and others. With so many people offering so many ideas, it was difficult to get them all to agree on anything, even where to put the visitor center.

In developing the design, Bob spent a lot of time visiting the proposed site. He would try to imagine exactly how the building might fit within and best utilize the area's natural features.

The three strongest features—the basin, the volcanoes, and the lake itself—were circular. So were the dwellings built by the Mono Lake Paiutes. Thus, it was decided that the shape of the visitor center would be circular, to blend in with the natural surroundings.

Bob eventually got everybody to agree on his design, and in January 1988 he showed it to Gordon and two of his architects, Gary Jereczek and Sam Nunes.

Gary and Sam began refining Bob's design. They wanted the major components of the building to be constructed with materials found in the sur-

Gary and Bob tried to envision the center in its environment before they began the actual design work.

rounding area, such as stones from a nearby quarry. They started to imagine the roofs and windows, and how many stories the building might be. The design team eventually narrowed down the many options and developed the overall building dimensions.

With several designs sketched out, it was time for the design team to present its plan to the members of the Forest Service. At the meeting, the GHC+A design team proposed a major change from the original concept, which had been an amorphous structure that lacked clarity of focus. They suggested the use of a cruciform, a cross-shaped structure, across the ceiling, as a central element of the building. They argued that one of the benefits of using the cruciform was to get more light into the center of the building. It would also give the structure more organization, and a cleaner shape.

SAM EDWARD NUNES

AGE: 34
PLACE OF BIRTH: San Jose, California
EDUCATIONAL BACKGROUND: B.A. in architecture, California Polytechnic State University, San Luis Obispo
POSITION: architect, project manager
JOINED GHC+A: 1984

Sam first stumbled on the office of GHC+A as he was heading to a gallery. "I had a portfolio with me because [as a recent college graduate] I was looking for work," Sam recalled. "I asked if they were hiring, and they looked at my portfolio. Then I met with Gordon. He offered me a job that day."

Sam has stayed with GHC+A for eleven years because the company has allowed him to develop his talents. At the age of twenty-eight, he was given the responsibility of putting together four- and five-million-dollar projects. In 1990, Sam became one of the firm's leading architects, along with Gary Jereczek.

Sam recalled the first time he was handed the reins of a major project and how that boosted his confidence. Several architects had recently left GHC+A, and Gordon turned to Sam to handle a $13.5 million project: converting a warehouse into the offices of Bancroft-Whitney Publishing Company. It was GHC+A's biggest project to date.

"I was the only one left from

the initial design team, and Gordon said, 'It's all on you. Let's get it done,' and I was able to do it," Sam said. "From there on, it was clear he had confidence in what I could do."

Sam credits Dick Osborne, former head architect at GHC+A, and Gordon for helping him achieve his career goals, "Dick more for the direct mentorship and the furthering of my appreciation of what it is to be an architect, and Gordon more for developing my understanding of the process."

Sam said the key to his success is that "people can believe in me. I try to be straight with every body. One of the skills that I bring to a team is the ability to communicate with a client."

Sam draws inspiration from a number of sources, among them other professionals, friends, and family. "My father has strength of character and carries himself with integrity," he said. "My mother has endless compassion. Their ability to support and encourage is unwavering. Both my parents come from very poor backgrounds. My dad drove a truck for fourteen hours a day and my mom worked in fruit canneries to earn the money to give their children opportunities."

It was not an easy sell. Many people at the meeting were reluctant to make the change. They liked their old design better. As Sam explained some of the problems with the original design, he could hear grumbling in the crowd. No one could agree on a design that night.

The team returned to San Francisco and continued to work on the design. They tried to address some of the concerns they had just heard. For instance, many people thought the building would rise too high, so the team lowered the roof.

Sam and Gary built three different models of the visitor center: one that represented the original idea, one full cruciform model, and one that blended the two ideas. They also drew more sketches, and Gary even made several airbrush paintings. They were now ready to make their final presentation.

The next meeting was held at the headquarters of the supervisor of the

It took hours of meetings to get a final design for the center approved.

Inyo National Forest in Bishop, a small town located about one hour south of Mono Lake. Attending the meeting were the supervisor and his staff and the district ranger for the Mono Basin Scenic Area.

Gordon decided he would accompany the design team and make a personal appeal for the cruciform design his architects had developed. At the meeting, Gordon and Bob Sandusky made a strong argument for the cruciform design. Some people, however, were still undecided. Nearly three hours passed before the design team was given approval to proceed with their idea.

The team flew back to San Francisco that night, excited that they would be able to develop their design. Back at the office, they worked on a final version of the cruciform model and made more detailed drawings, called *schematics*.

This shot of the completed visitor center shows how the cruciform design and high windows give the building a cathedral-like quality.

The cruciform design divided the building into four distinct sections. Each section would house one of the four major areas: the exhibit space, theater, gallery, and store. The design also helped identify the traffic patterns through the building.

The cruciform rose high above the circular forms of the building. The cross-shaped form and high windows gave the building an uplifting, cathedral-like quality. One of the purposes of a cathedral's design is to help a person move from this world to the world of God. The visitor center's similarity to a cathedral seemed appropriate to the architects. At the visitor center, the idea is to reorient people to nature and the environment.

When the design team gave their final presentation at a public hearing in Lee Vining several months later, their design was well received.

The next step in designing the visitor center was deciding on the building materials and developing the plans for heating, cooling, electrical, and other systems. This stage usually marks the final step in the design process.

Sam and Gary now selected the color of the stone, the type of wood, as well as the lighting and plumbing fixtures to be used in the center. They chose fitted pumice from a local quarry and sunset "misty mauve" colors to heighten the feeling of natural splendor. They decided to leave the wood exposed and unpainted. They left the concrete floors bare. They opted for high windows that let in lots of natural light. The building would have more than 200 windows and ten glass doors.

The roofing material for the visitor center would have to withstand 100-mile-per-hour winds, heavy snow loads, and excessive heat. Working closely with three of the firm's engineers—Paul Westermann, Tom Bowers, and Renee Rabigea—Gary and Sam evaluated different materials to see which ones would best meet their building's needs and budget. They ended up choosing a metal and synthetic slate roof.

The engineers then made drawings to illustrate all of the heating, ventilating, and air-conditioning systems for the building. The drawings included plumbing and ductwork details. The engineers also drew the electrical system. These drawings showed all the wiring, light fixtures, and outlets in the building. Then Gary designed the theater and projection rooms.

When Gary and Sam were through, the building enclosed 13,300 square feet, most of which were on the ground floor and would be open to the public. The administrative offices, library, laboratory, workroom, and mechanical systems (such as boilers, fuse boxes, etc.) were situated on a lower level. On the grounds, they put in two parking lots, one for automobiles and one for recreational vehicles and buses. The grounds also included a one-half-mile nature trail, two acres of groomed landscaping, an information kiosk, and a patio with native pumice walls and redwood benches.

Once the building materials were chosen and the systems were designed, the next task was to create what are called *construction documents*. The drawings and specifications in these documents tell the contractor exactly how to

The natural materials used in the center's interior are a perfect match with its purpose: to educate visitors about the history of the land on which they stand.

COMPUTERS AT WORK

Computers are revolutionizing the architectural services industry. Recognized as valuable tools for the architect, 88 percent of architecture firms are now computerized, with the few remaining firms being solo practitioners. In fact, in the last five years, the use of personal computers has more than doubled. An estimated 47,000 personal computers are now in use in architectural firms across the country.

Word processing is the most common use for computers, but the number of firms using computer-aided design and drafting (CAD) is growing. In 1994, more than half of all firms were using CAD and another 19 percent anticipated purchasing a CAD system.

CAD has been around more

than twenty years, but in its early days it was used only by large firms that could afford very expensive mainframe computers. In the last ten years, with the arrival of moderately priced PCs and architectural software, smaller firms have also been able to use CAD.

At Gordon H Chong + Associates, architect Eric McKinney has been promoting greater use of computers in every aspect of the business. When he joined the firm in 1986, it had a few PCs. Eric brought in a Macintosh to demonstrate to his colleagues some of its uses.

Today, GHC+A has about thirty personal computer work stations and eighteen CAD stations—all networked together. These computers are used in both administrative and design work. They make it easier to write letters, calculate fees, organize information, and manage money or other numbers.

They also help architects communicate through drawings.

John Ruffo, who oversees the computers with Eric, estimates that about 80 percent of the firm's architectural work is now done on CAD. Using CAD, architects can tell contractors precisely what they are thinking. Furthermore, "many clients require it," said John. "It's better for the long-term documentation of a facility, it's more efficient, and it's more accurate. The documents look better and cleaner."

But, in the early stages of the design process, the pencil and paper are still the preference because it offers a looser, more flexible feel than CAD. It's also quicker. "Clients don't like to see computer drawings in the beginning because they feel too permanent," said Ruffo. "I don't think that will ever change."

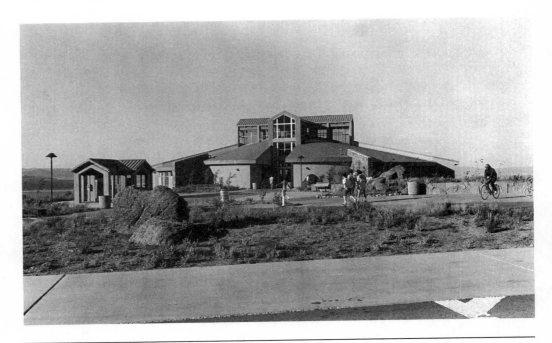

The finished center appears to rise naturally out of the ground.

build the building. Gary and Sam, along with engineers Paul, Tom, and Renee, produced drawings that showed how the many materials would connect, how the concrete would get reinforced with steel, and how the building would attach to its foundation.

In most architectural projects, the architectural firm usually oversees the construction process once a contractor is selected to build the structure. This is known as construction administration. In the case of the Mono Lake Visitor Center, however, the U.S. Forest Service managed the construction administration because it was a public project. Construction of the building began in 1990 and was completed in 1991.

The Mono Basin National Forest Scenic Area Visitor Center, located on Highway 395 just north of Lee Vining, opened on May 20, 1992. It was a grand ceremony, attended by local politicians, people from the U.S. Forest Service, the Mono Lake Committee, and GHC+A. Even officials from the Los Angeles Department of Power and Water were on hand.

Thousands of visitors pass through the center's exhibits each year.

It was a beautiful afternoon. The Forest Service officials thanked Bob Sandusky and the architects of Gordon H Chong + Associates for their work. People gave speeches about the fight to protect Mono Lake, and a Mono Paiute woman said a prayer in her native tongue.

The visitor center was dedicated to the memory of David Gaines, who had led the fight to save Mono land and had died in 1988 in a winter automobile accident near Lee Vining. People compared Gaines to John Muir and others who were instrumental in preserving California's natural landscape.

Visitors can use interactive exhibits to learn Mono Lake's history.

Some visitors sit outside and just enjoy the view. Inside or out, they're sure to enjoy all the center has to offer.

Since the opening, visitors have passed through the center daily. A variety of activities and exhibits, including a twenty-minute film, an interactive exhibit hall, two art galleries, and a bookstore, introduce them to the natural and human history of the Mono Basin. As they enter the vestibule into the main space, they are struck by the image of the lake. People stare through the glass at the vast expanse of blue water before them. Framed by the dramatic architecture, the majestic lake and its two islands become a unified work of art.

Conclusion: New Challenges

In the architectural industry, only 6 percent of the firms consist of twenty or more people. GHC+A has sixty-three. Yet the *Engineering News Record,* which recently ranked the top 500 design firms nationwide, rated number 500 as being 50 percent larger (in billing) than GHC+A is currently! This points up how difficult it is for a midsize firm, even a successful one like GHC+A, to be in the mainstream of the profession.

"You either have to be very large or very small," said Gordon. "My own interest is in doing more complex projects, which doesn't permit us to be smaller. We're at an awkward size right now."

As the firm grows, one of the greatest pressures will be to keep the jobs coming in. And because it no longer receives preferences as a small minority-owned firm, the challenge to attract more business is even greater.

Gordon believes he can succeed in bringing in new projects in several ways.

"If we had a direction, I'd say in five or ten years, we would be larger and more diverse geographically, maybe with offices in locations other than San Francisco," he said.

That will mean setting up branch offices around California, as well as regional offices outside California and continuing to build on the expertise the firm has already developed.

"I'm interested in continuing to do hospital work, university work, and more civic buildings," said Gordon. "If there's opportunity to do more airport work, we'll do that."

Gordon will also begin developing additional services. For instance, the firm now has a new group of interior-design architects. Gordon is also considering hiring his own person to do cost estimating of projects, a service he usually pays an outside consultant to handle.

As the firm grows, it must also safeguard against potential problems. Gordon is cautious when it comes to growth. He wants to make sure that the firm does not grow too fast and that it has a chance to regroup.

Today, it is more important than ever before to remain flexible. To get jobs and keep everyone working, the firm will have to be faster to respond to changing conditions in the economy and the marketplace.

As the firm grows, it will also be necessary to increase the management staff, and broaden ownership of the firm. And as it gets bigger, it is important that the firm not become too bureaucratic. "We don't want to lose what has gotten us where we are," said Linda Crouse. "We want to use the culture of the firm to propel us forward."

The culture, she said, is "our energy, our open communication, our willingness to change direction, and to not be set in our ways."

The profession today is very different than it was when Gordon started out. California schools of architecture are represented by large numbers of minority students. When these students become practicing architects, the leadership of the profession could change significantly. Gordon said, "We need to be much better in the next generation, thus our focus on growing."

Glossary

affirmative action—a program designed to address past discrimination against a specific group of people by giving them the first opportunity at a job or project.

air-conditioning—the process of treating air so as to control its temperature, humidity, and cleanliness within an interior space.

architect—an individual trained and licensed to design and oversee the construction of buildings.

architect-engineer—an individual offering professional services as both architect and engineer.

architecture—the art and science of designing and building structures.

beam—a construction element made of wood or metal whose prime function is as a horizontal support in a structure.

blueprint—a reproduction of architectural or working drawings. The typical blueprint has a white background and black or blue lines.

civil engineer—an engineer trained in the design of structures such as buildings, roads, tunnels, and bridges.

construction—all the on-site work done in building or in altering structures.

construction documents—the working drawings and specifications.

consultant—an individual engaged by a firm on a limited basis to provide professional services in his or her area of expertise. A consultant is paid by the hour or by the project, but is not a salaried employee.

contractor—one who performs or supervises construction work, including providing labor and materials, in accordance with plans provided by the architect.

draftsman—a person who draws building plans and construction documents.

ducts—pipes or tubes, round or rectangular, designed to carry the air in heating, ventilating, or air-conditioning systems.

electrical engineer—the engineer responsible for designing the electrical service of a building.

interior design—the art or practice of decorating and furnishing the inside of structures.

landscape architect—a person trained and experienced in the design and development of outdoor features, especially around building sites. These features include not just vegetation but also lighting and irrigation systems.

loft—a large, open upper floor of a building.

marketing director—the person in a firm responsible for promoting the firm and its work to potential clients.

mechanical engineer—the engineer responsible for ensuring that a structure is supplied with all necessary conditioned air and water.

model—a representation or reproduction, usually on a small scale, to illustrate construction.

portfolio—a portable case of sample drawings and papers, showing the work the person or firm has done.

principal—a person legally responsible for the activities of the firm.

scale drawing—a drawing that is in proportion to the actual object it represents but whose size is greatly reduced.

schematics—detailed drawings that illustrate the scale and relationship of the project's components.

site—an area or plot of ground on which a building is to be located.

specifications—written instructions to the contractor on the work to be done, the material to be used, and the method by which the work is to be carried out. *Specifications* are a part of the construction documents.

structural engineer—the engineer responsible for designing the basic supporting elements of the building, including the foundation and the frame.

urban planning—planning a community, taking into account such factors as convenience to residents, environmental conditions, societal needs, and economic constraints.

For More Information

The American Institute of Architects
1735 New York Avenue, N.W.
Washington, DC 20006
(202) 626-7300

Asian American Architects and
    Engineers
c/o Asian, Inc.
1670 Pine Street
San Francisco, CA 94109
(415) 928-5910

Asian Business League
233 Sansome Street, Suite 1102
San Francisco, CA 94104
(415) 788-4664

Asian Neighborhood Design
461 Bush Street, Suite 400
San Francisco, CA 94108
(415) 982-2959

Chinatown Resource Center
1525 Grant Avenue
San Francisco, CA 94133
(415) 984-1454

Chinese Culture Foundation of San
    Francisco
750 Kearny Street
San Francisco, CA 94108
(415) 986-1822

LEAP
165 10th Street
San Francisco, CA 94103
(415) 861-1899

New York Chinatown History
    Museum
70 Mulberry Street
New York, NY 10013
(212) 619-4785

For Further Reading

Adkins, Jan. *How a House Happens.* New York: Walker, 1972.

———. *Toolchest.* New York: Walker, 1973.

Barton, Byron. *Building a House.* New York: Greenwillow, 1981.

Biesty, Stephen. *Stephen Biesty's Incredible Cross-sections.* New York: Random House, 1992.

Dobrin, Peter. *Start Exploring Architecture: A Fact-Filled Coloring Book.* Philadelphia: Runing Press, 1993.

Donati, Paolo. *Amazing Buildings.* Boston: Houghton Mifflin, 1993.

Eisen, David. *Fun with Architecture: From the Metropolitan Museum of Art.* New York: Viking, 1992.

Eyewitness Visual Dictionaries. *The Visual Dictionary of Buildings.* Boston: Houghton Mifflin/Dorling Kindersley, 1992.

Gibbons, Gail. *Up Goes the Skyscraper!* New York: Four Winds Press, 1986.

Giblin, James. *Let There Be Light: A Book About Windows.* New York: Crowell, 1988.

Isaacson, Philip M. *Round Buildings, Square Buildings, and Buildings that Wiggle like Fish.* New York: Random House, 1988.

Korab, Balthazar. *Archabet; an Architectural Alphabet.* Washington, D.C.: Preservation Press, 1985.

Loup, Jean Jacques. *The Architect.* Woodbury, N.Y.: Barrons, 1977.

Macaulay, David. *Castle.* Boston: Houghton Mifflin, 1977.

———. *Cathedral; the Story of Its Construction.* Boston: Houghton Mifflin, 1973.

————. *City; a Story of Roman Planning and Construction*. Boston: Houghton Mifflin, 1974.

————. *Mill*. Boston: Houghton Mifflin, 1983.

————. *Pyramid*. Boston: Houghton Mifflin, 1975.

————. *Unbuilding*. Boston: Houghton Mifflin, 1980.

————. *Underground*. Boston: Houghton Mifflin, 1976.

McGraw, Sheila. *This Old New House*. Loganville, GA.: Firefly, 1988.

Salvadori, Mario. *The Art of Construction*. Chicago: Chicago Review Press, 1990.

Stern, Robert A. M. *The House that Bob Built*. New York: Rizzoli, 1991.

von Tscharner, Tenata, and Fleming, Ronald Lee. *New Providence: A Changing Cityscape*. Washington, D.C.: Preservation Press, 1988.

Wilson, Forrest. *What It Feels Like to Be a Building*. Washington, D.C.: Preservation Press, 1988.

Index

Page numbers in italics refer to boxed features.

77

DATE DUE

PIGEONS

BY MIRIAM SCHLEIN

PHOTOGRAPHS BY

MARGARET MILLER

THOMAS Y. CROWELL

NEW YORK

Photo credits: The Bettmann Archive, 28; Mike Brown, *Florida Today*, 32; Culver Pictures, Inc., 27, 29 (bottom), 30, 37 (top), 38 (bottom), 39; *Egyptian Travel Magazine*, Egyptian Tourist Administration, 26; Magnum Photos, Inc., photo by Elliott Erwitt, 33; New York Zoological Society Photo: 37 (bottom), 38 (top); Miriam Schlein, 19 (top), 24 (bottom); U.S. Army Military History Institute, 29, (top), 31 (both).

Pigeons

Library of Congress Cataloging-in-Publication Data
Schlein, Miriam.
    Pigeons.

    Summary: Explains how pigeons—descendants of wild rock doves—live their lives, raise their young, and have been useful throughout history to people.
    1. Pigeons. [1. Pigeons] I. Miller, Margaret, 1945– ill. II. Title.
QL 696.C63S35   1989   598'.65   88-35286
ISBN 0-690-04808-4
ISBN 0-690-04810-6 (lib. bdg.)

Typography by Christine Kettner
1   2   3   4   5   6   7   8   9   10
First Edition

PIGEONS

In the city, there are pigeons all around. They march in little bunches along the sidewalk. They sit in rows on rooftops. They love to sit on statues.

Wherever you look, there they are. You can hear them, too.

Coo-roo...coo-roo.

5

Why do pigeons live in the city? You would think that birds would want to live where there are more trees.

City pigeons are descendants of wild rock doves, birds that nest high on cliffs and rock ledges.

Look around. Tall city buildings are like man-made "cliffs." And there are all kinds of ledges where pigeons can perch. Windowsills. Bridge beams. Steeples, towers, roofs. The pigeons feel at home. To them, the city is a natural place to live.

Because there are so many pigeons around, we take them for granted. We don't pay much attention to them. But watch them. You can see pigeons do some interesting things.

7

Close-up of a city pigeon

A city pigeon is about 11 inches long and weighs about 10 ounces. Most are gray, with a ring of glossy green and purple feathers around the neck. Some are black. A few are light brown, or creamy white with brown specks. Sometimes you see an all-white one.

8

Their heads bob back and forth as they walk. Their little round eyes are red or yellow, and shine like glassy beads.

9

See the small white lump at the base of the bill? This is called the *cere*. It's tough flesh, like a callus. It protects the nose slits.

10

Pigeon toes are long, red, and skinny. Curled around, they get a firm grip on any edge.

Sometimes you see what looks like a one-legged pigeon. But it may not be. The pigeon could be just standing on one foot. The other leg is pulled up to rest and is hidden in the feathers.

11

You might see pigeons taking a bath in a puddle. They flap their wings and ruffle their feathers so the water seeps in. When they get out, they flap some more to shed water, then sit in the sun to dry off.

In a snowstorm, if they have no shelter, they just brave it out. They sit on a ledge, hunched over, facing inward, and wait for the storm to end.

You might see a pigeon standing on the ground flapping its wings but not taking off. What's it doing? It's exercising, to keep its wing muscles in shape.

The wings are pointy; the tail is straight-edged. In flight, it spreads out like a fan. The down-flap of the wings moves the pigeon ahead; the feathers are tight together. On the up-flap, the feathers are spread, to let the air through.

The tail is used to steer and brake.

Pigeons have keen eyesight. But they can't see straight ahead from a distance. Pigeon eyes work separately—one eye looks to the left side, one to the right. In flight, this helps them see an enemy approaching.

Close up, they *can* see straight ahead. Sometimes, to look at something, they cock their head to one side.

They are certainly not fussy eaters. They eat stuff they find lying around—crumbs, a bit of cheese, a shred of meat from a sandwich. They don't have a keen sense of taste. (We have 9,000 taste buds in our mouth. A pigeon has only 37.)

This doesn't mean they'll eat any old thing. Sometimes you'll see a pigeon pick something up and drop it three or four times before eating it.

The pigeon is testing—trying to figure out whether the thing is okay to eat. They judge by the feel of it. And if they do happen to eat something that makes them sick—say, a certain kind of berry—they will never eat that same kind of thing again.

They eat a lot, very fast. They have a special pouch in

15

their throat, called the *crop*, where food is stored.

Sometimes you see pigeons pecking up sand and pebbles. They do this for a special reason. The pebbles go to a part of their stomach called the *gizzard*. Here, the pebbles roll around and help crush food.

Pigeons drink in an unusual way. They suck water up fast, like they're

16

using a straw. Other birds don't drink that way. Other birds take one sip at a time, each time lifting the head to swallow, then bending down for another sip.

The pigeon is the only bird that feeds its babies milk. Pigeon milk comes from the parent's crop. It's like milk with little cheeselike lumps in it. To get fed, the chick sticks its bill (and whole head, practically) into its parent's mouth. Both mother and father pigeons give pigeon milk.

People say, "There are so many pigeons. Why don't I ever see any baby pigeons?"

It's true. Most pigeons lay their eggs in hidden-away places. But sometimes they make a nest where you can see it. If you are lucky, you may have a chance to watch a mother and father pigeon bring up their babies.

17

Notes of a pigeon-watcher

Two pigeons are hanging around a lot on a windowsill across the way. They coo, and nibble each other's necks.

Soon they get very busy. They fly back and forth, carrying twigs. They pile them up. They're making a nest. Are they going to have a family?

From now on, every time I look, there's always a pigeon sitting in that spot. . . .

This is a good sign there may be eggs there. A mother pigeon lays two eggs, each weighing half an ounce. You hardly ever see pigeon eggs, because usually either the mother or father pigeon is sitting on them, to incubate them (keep them warm).

18

They take regular shifts. The mother sits from late afternoon through the night. In the morning, the father takes over and sits through the day.

After about 17 days, the eggs hatch. The babies peck their way out.

First week

I look out. It happened! There are two baby chicks. They're poking out from under the big pigeon. They're very small. They're covered with yellow fuzz.

As I watch, the big pigeon bends down and puts its beak right around a baby's mouth and head. The big one is feeding the baby pigeon milk. Then it feeds the second one.

When the feeding is over, the big one totally covers the babies with its body. If you looked out now, you wouldn't know the

19

babies were there. Now, all you can see is a big pigeon, sitting....

Second week

The chicks are bigger. They're losing their yellow fuzz. They're skinny and bald-looking now. Most of the time they sit close together, side by side. They have little round eyes. Do they see me looking at them?

They're alone now, a lot of the time. The mother and father keep coming back to feed them. But they stay only a short time. One parent is dusky black. The other is brown with a white head and tail. I wonder: Which is the mother, which is the father? Dusky-black is a bit bigger. Maybe he's the father.

The chicks are growing fast. They have some feathers now.

20

But under their wings, their skin is still bald-looking. They walk around now, in a sort of crouch. They lift their wings a bit. It's as though their wings feel heavy.

Now that they have feathers, I can tell them apart. One chick is solid brown. The other has a white head.

Third week

The chicks compete to get fed first. Each one tries to push the other away. White-head usually wins out. Sometimes there doesn't seem to be anything left for Brownie.

White-head stands facing inward doing fast practice wing-flaps. He can't fly yet. I guess he faces in so he doesn't take off by mistake. How does he know to face in?

Brownie just sits. She hasn't

21

done any wing-flaps yet. I worry. Is she getting enough to eat?

Here comes Dusky-black Pop, in for a feeding. Brownie stretches out her wings, keeping White-head back. For once, she has outmaneuvered him. This time, she's getting firsts on food. "Come on, Brownie," I whisper.

Feeding is pretty frantic. The chick's bill and part of its head are in Dusky-black Pop's mouth. The heads of parent and chick go up and down in a pumping motion. Their bodies quiver and shake. A bit of food dribbles down between their mouths.

Fourth week

Brownie's doing okay. She has tried a few wing-flaps. The chicks are now as tall as the parents. But not as plump.

Here comes White-head Mom.

22

The chicks bang at her with their wings. They peck her on the head. She scoots to the other end of the ledge. She gives a little burp. Then she turns back to feed them. Those pigeon parents are really something. She could have flown off when then were bopping and pecking at her. But she didn't. . . .

Milk is made in the parents' crops for only about ten days. So the chicks are not getting pigeon milk anymore. Now they're being fed regurgitated food.

The chicks don't look so macho today. It's raining hard. They're huddled together. They look bedraggled and drippy.

Fifth week
This is it! Brownie's alone.

23

White-head has flown off. I hope he makes it on his own.

Brownie looks lonely. But she's not deserted. White-head Mom and Dusky-black Pop keep coming back to feed her. At night, the three roost together on the ledge.

Next day

I look out. Well, well. Brownie's gone, too. The ledge is empty. I've been watching them for more than a month. I guess I won't ever see them again. I hope they both lead good pigeon lives. . . .

The day after that

Dusky-black Pop is sitting in the corner. White-head Mom is nibbling around his head. They both look tired. No wonder. They really worked hard, bringing up their babies.

❧

From September to November pigeons *molt*. Old feathers fall out. New ones grow in. Soon the pigeons will start a new family.

Male pigeons are slightly larger than female; their neck feathers are a bit more shiny.

When a pigeon coos, often it's to keep in touch with its mate, who may be nearby but out of sight.

When pigeons are courting, a whole lot of cooing goes on. The male pigeon struts around the female. His crop is blown up, his feathers ruffled. The female sticks her beak into his. He feeds her regurgitated food. This is called "billing." It's a sign the pigeons are going to mate.

Pigeon pairs stay together for life. Often, they raise 5 or 6 or even more broods (families) a year.

A young pigeon is sometimes called a *squab*. If a pigeon stays healthy, it might live for 10 years or more.

Heroes, Helpers, Homers

Pigeons are very fast flyers. Some have been clocked at more than 90 miles per hour in races. (They can do this when there is a good tailwind to help them.) And they are especially good at finding their way home from hundreds, even thousands, of miles away.

In ancient days, when people learned about these special abilities that pigeons have, they put pigeons to work. In Greece, Rome, Egypt, and Persia, pigeons regularly carried news and messages from one city to another.

One emperor in India had 20,000 letter-carrying pigeons so he could

Egyptian carrier pigeons, about 45 B.C.

26

keep in touch with officials all over his empire.

In Greece, when the first Olympics were held in *776* B.C., how did people all over Greece find out who the winners were? Pigeons carried the news.

In 1815, how did the people of England first find out that their army had defeated Napoleon at the Battle of Waterloo? They got the news by carrier pigeon.

Banks in Paris and Brussels used to send stock market reports out by "Exchange Pigeons." In fact, until the telegraph (1836) and telephone (1875) were invented, the fastest way to send any kind of news was by pigeon.

Pigeons have even been honored as war heroes.

Carrier pigeon, 1871.

In World War I, a pigeon named Cher Ami ("dear friend" in French) saved the lives of many men of the "Lost Battalion," part of New York's 77th Division. During a battle in the Argonne Forest in France, they were cut off from the rest of the Allied troops and surrounded by the enemy. They were being fired on by their own artillery, who didn't know they were there.

They tried to get help. The first message they sent out was: "Many wounded. We cannot evacuate." But the pigeon carrying the message was shot down.

The second message was: "Men are suffering. Can support be sent…?" That pigeon didn't make it either.

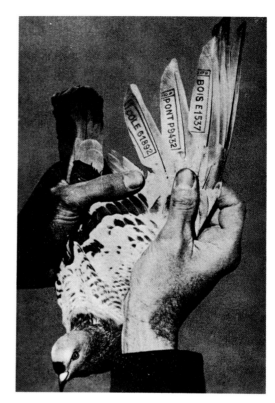

French carrier pigeon with war message on its feathers, 1914. (*Pont* means bridge; *Bois* means forest. The meaning of *Cole* is not known.)

They had one homing pigeon left—Cher Ami. The message was: "Our artillery is dropping a barrage on us. For heaven's sake, stop it!" Cher Ami was released. He was their last hope. As the men watched, they saw him shot down. But in a moment, he got up. As he flew over enemy fire, he had a leg shot off, and was shot in the breast. But he kept going. When he arrived, his feathers were covered with blood. But he got the message through, and saved lives.

At the end of the war, Cher Ami and more than 40 other pigeon heroes were sent back to the United States on the USS *Ohioan*. They were well cared for until they died. Cher Ami's body has been

Cher Ami

World War I homing pigeons. Sign on cage reads: "MILITARY HOMING PIGEONS. These are the birds that work to save the lives of our boys in France."

29

U.S. soldiers releasing carrier pigeons, 1943.

preserved and is now at the Smithsonian Institution in Washington, D.C.

In World War II, a British fishing boat was attacked by a German submarine. One of the crew members had a pet on board—a homing pigeon. As the boat was sinking, the wounded skipper attached a message to the pigeon: *"Nelson* attacked by subs. Send assistance." Skipper Crisp died on board. But the pigeon got the message through, and crew members were picked up. Skipper Crisp was posthumously awarded the Victoria Cross (the VC) for bravery. The pigeon was named after him, and called Crisp, VC.

In World War II, spies who parachuted behind enemy lines would

30

have a pigeon tied to their chest. Later, the pigeon was sent back with intelligence information.

Advance foot patrols also took pigeons with them. When they learned about enemy positions, they sent word back by pigeon.

Army pigeons wore a leather harness. The message was in a tube attached to the harness. When the pigeon was flying, you couldn't see its tube or harness. It looked like just a wild bird. Sometimes the message was put in a small container attached to the pigeon's leg.

Right now, pigeons are saving lives in peacetime, too. They are trained in search-and-rescue operations to find ship and plane survivors in

Army carrier pigeon wearing a harness.

Aluminum message capsule

31

the sea. With their keen eyesight, pigeons are better able than people to spot the orange speck of a lifejacket.

The pigeons are kept in a special compartment in the search helicopter. When they see something, they peck at a keyboard. A light lights up. The copter pilot goes down. Pigeons can spot a survivor 90 percent of the time. People can do it only 40 percent of the time.

In a fishing village on a small island off the coast of France, there is a doctor, but no medical laboratory. When a blood test or some other test has to be done, the doctor sends the sample by pigeon to the mainland, where it is examined in a lab. The pigeon wears a vest. The vial with the sample is carried in a little vest pocket.

In May 1987, a pigeon helped a news photographer get a "scoop." While President and Nancy Reagan attended the memorial service for sailors who had died in the attack on the USS *Stark*, for security reasons no reporters were allowed to leave the naval station. But there was no rule against a pigeon leaving!

Photographer Robert Self brought a homing pigeon in with him—a 2-year-old, 14-ounce gray female who had won some 400-mile races. Self took his photos, attached the film to the pigeon's leg,

Robert Self removes pigeon from box to attach film capsule.

32

and set her free. An hour later, the pigeon returned home. This is how the *Jacksonville* (Florida) *Journal* got its photo before any other newspaper.

And so even now, in these days of jet planes, phones, and computers, sometimes the best way to send information is still by pigeon.

How do homing pigeons find their way home?

First, they circle around to get their bearings. Then they look at the sun. Scientists believe that pigeons can tell direction by the position of the sun in the sky.

When the sun is not visible, pigeons may be able to use the earth's magnetic field to help guide them. It's been discovered that pigeons have a bit of *magnetite* in their heads. This is the mineral from which the first

magnetic compasses were made. It is possible that this helps pigeons in their homing ability. In other words, each pigeon may carry its own compass right in its body. There is no proof of this as yet.

(It's interesting that salmon and monarch butterflies, who also do pinpoint navigation, have magnetite in their bodies, too.)

Many people raise homing pigeons, and race them as a hobby. The pigeons live in a *loft*, usually on the roof. This is the way they're trained: The owner first takes them one mile away, then two miles, then to more and more distant places before releasing them. Like any athlete, the pigeons improve with practice. Soon they are ready to race.

The pigeons are taken to a place miles from home. (There are 60-, 100-, and 400-mile races, or longer.) Each pigeon has a band with a number attached to its leg. They are released all at the same time.

Meanwhile, the owners have gone back home. When a pigeon returns, it enters the loft through a trapdoor. The owner takes the numbered leg band off and puts it into a special timing box that records the exact time of arrival.

Not all lofts are exactly the same distance from the start. So the winner is the pigeon that has reached home at the fastest average speed—not the one that gets back first.

From how far away can a homing pigeon find its way

35

back? This story will give us an idea.

A man in Long Island, New York, gave a "homer" to a friend who lived in Venezuela in South America. When the South American returned home, he let the New York pigeon out with the rest of his flock. This pigeon never came back with the others. The man thought it had been eaten by hawks, or had gotten lost. But the pigeon wasn't lost at all. It knew just where it was going! Three months later, it arrived back at its original home on Long Island. This was a flight of more than 2,000 miles.

Pigeons are in the family called *Columbidae* (from the Latin word *columba*, meaning dove). This family includes doves as well as pigeons. Usually, but not always, pigeons are larger than doves.

There are about 300 different species (types) of doves and pigeons. Not all live in cities. Some live in woods and fields. Fruit pigeons live in tropical forests.

They don't all look like city pigeons, either.

Tropical *fruit pigeons* are mostly green—good protective coloring for life in a tropical forest. Often they

Etching of the common pigeon from 1735.

have bright flecks of yellow or red. Some have many beautiful colors combined— yellow, orange, blue, green, and purple.

The *wood pigeon* is quite big—about 17 inches. It lives in the woods and eats buds, flowers, seeds, and leaves. It pecks up leaf bits at a rate of 100 per minute, often pecking up 35,000 bits in one day.

Tumbler pigeons do acrobatic loop-de-loops in the air.

The *pouter pigeon* puffs its neck out with air.

The *bleeding heart pigeon* of the Philippines has a red splotch on its breast that looks so much like blood that people who see it in a zoo often report an injured bird.

The *crowned pigeon* is the giant of pigeons. Some are as

Pouter pigeon

Bleeding heart pigeon

37

big as a turkey. It can measure 28 inches and weigh about 30 pounds. It lives in New Guinea and on Catalina Island, off the coast of California. It has a fanlike crest on its head.

Crowned pigeon

At one time, there were billions of beautiful gray-and-white *passenger pigeons*. Flocks were so large they blotted out the sun from view for days. John Audubon, the naturalist and artist, watched one flock that took three days to fly by. He estimated there were more than a billion birds in the flock.

Now there is not one passenger pigeon left in the world.

What happened?

They were too easy to kill.

Passenger pigeon

38

Landing, they were so thick in the trees, people could knock them off with a pole. People had "slaughtering parties." They killed passenger pigeons for fun. Billions were also killed to be sold as food for a penny apiece.

The last passenger pigeon was named Martha. She died in the Cincinnati Zoo in 1914.

Mass slaughter of passenger pigeons, 1867.

Have you ever heard the saying "dead as a dodo"? The dodo was a strange relative of the pigeon. It had a thick beak, stumpy wings, and an odd little curly-feathered tail. It was big; it weighed about 50 pounds. But it couldn't fly. It also was too easy to kill.

Dodoes used to live on islands off Africa. Like the passenger pigeon, it is now extinct.

Pigeons existed as long as two million years ago. We know this because fossils of pigeons have been found from those times. Now pigeons live in almost every part of the world except for Antarctica, the Arctic, and a few small islands.

Some pigeon words

pigeonhole: a small cubbyhole to put things in, usually on a desk (because pigeons squeeze into very small places)

stool pigeon: someone who betrays his friends (because people used to tie a pigeon to a stool as a decoy to attract other pigeons into a net to be trapped)

pigeon-toed: walking with your toes pointed inward

billing and cooing: two people acting very affectionate ("lovey-dovey") with each other (the way courting pigeons do)

Some people are fond of pigeons. They feed them seeds and crumbs. The pigeons get to know them. And even if the person is not throwing crumbs that day, the pigeons will still flock around.

Other people object to pigeons. Some farmers do, because pigeons eat grain. Some city people do, because of the mess caused by pigeon droppings. Pigeons can also carry disease. So watch them—but don't touch them, or pick them up.

City pigeons are survivors. Speedy, spunky, raising their families. Walking along in gangs, bobbing their heads as they walk. And making one of the nicest city sounds. Coo-roo…coo-roo…

A PIGEON ALBUM

Index

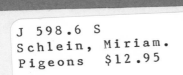